RESCUELOGIC®
SOFTWARE BY CADGRAPHICS®

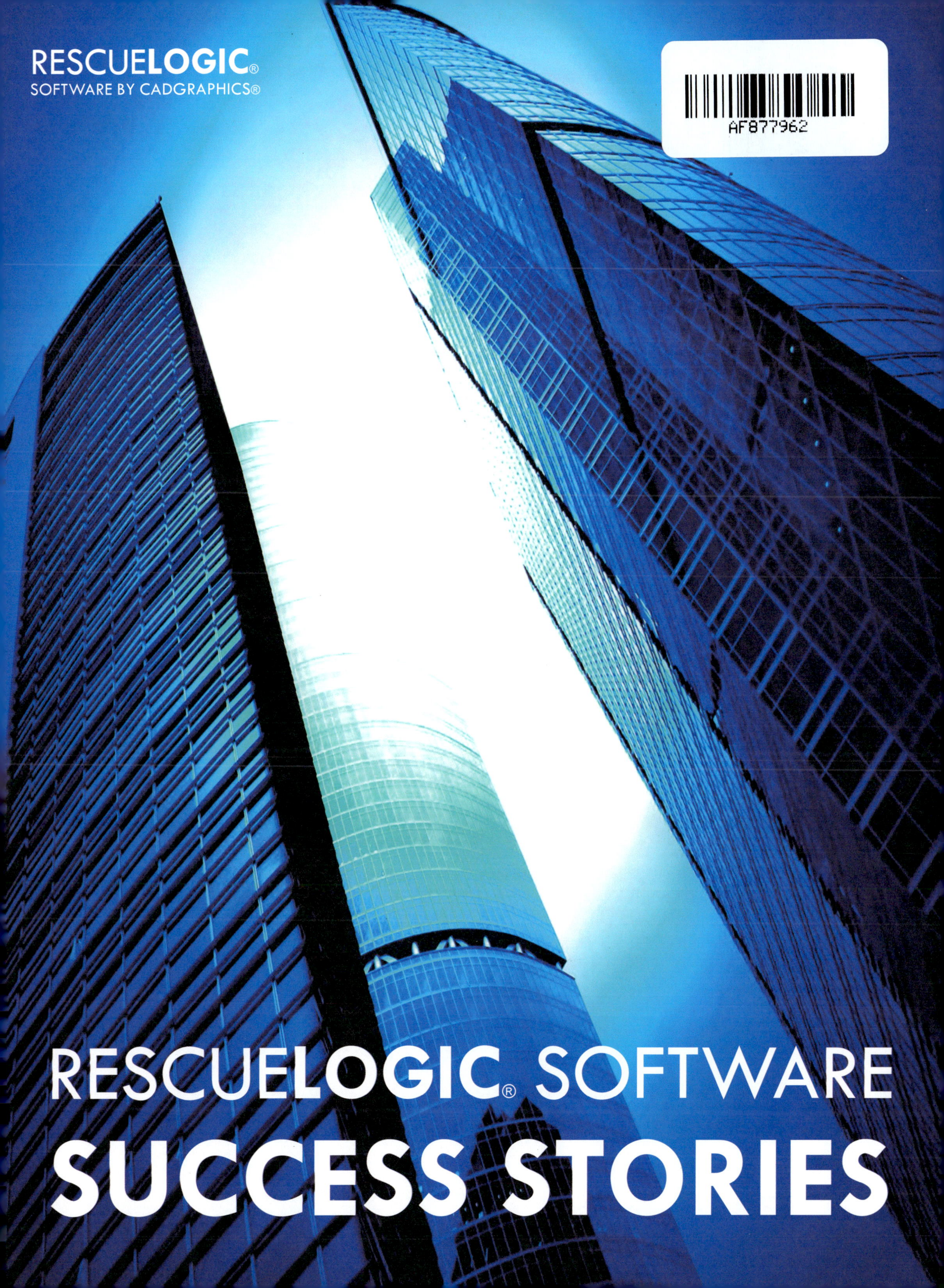

RESCUELOGIC® SOFTWARE SUCCESS STORIES

RESCUE**LOGIC**®
SOFTWARE BY CADGRAPHICS®

SUCCESS STORIES

RescueLogic puts YOU in control of your fire and security systems.

RescueLogic is "safety made simple."

Inside Stories

RESCUE**LOGIC**®
SOFTWARE BY CADGRAPHICS

Get a bird's-eye view of your fire and security system

Does your fire and security system work for you, or do you work for it? With RescueLogic software, you can see data from every alarm and device on your site, in a single, streamlined interface.

RescueLogic displays real-time information about those alarms and devices on maps, floor plans, and color-coded lists, along with correspon-ding "Take Action" messages.

If your job involves fire protection, security, facility management, or emergency response, then you need RescueLogic software.

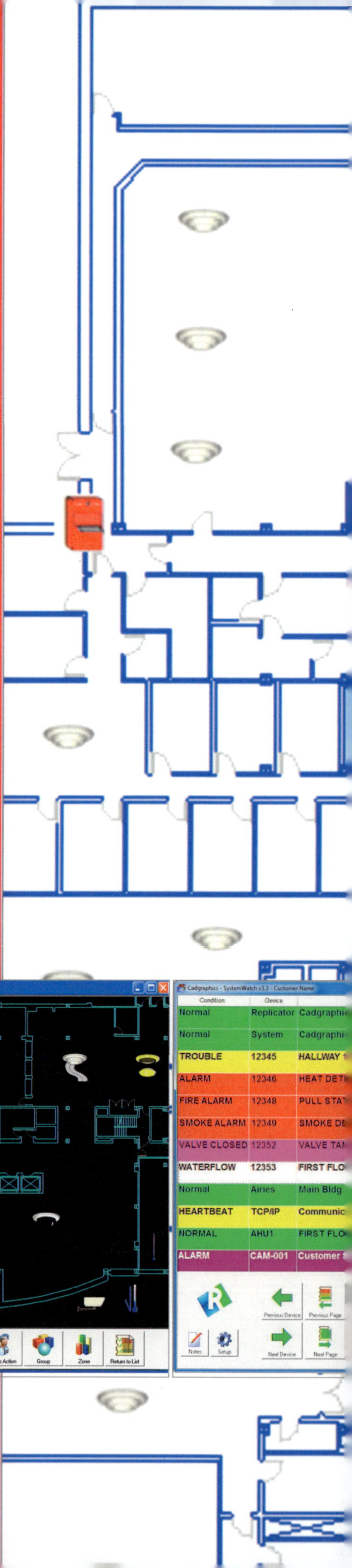

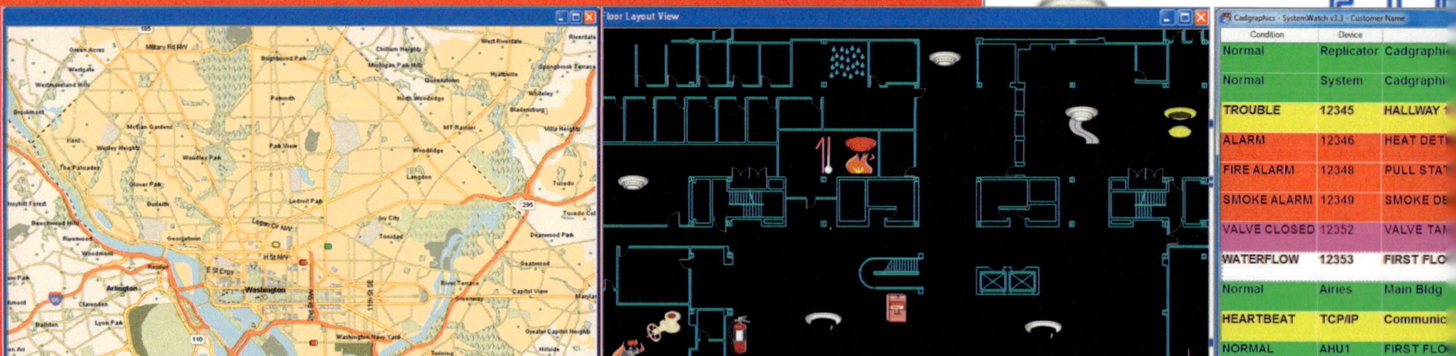

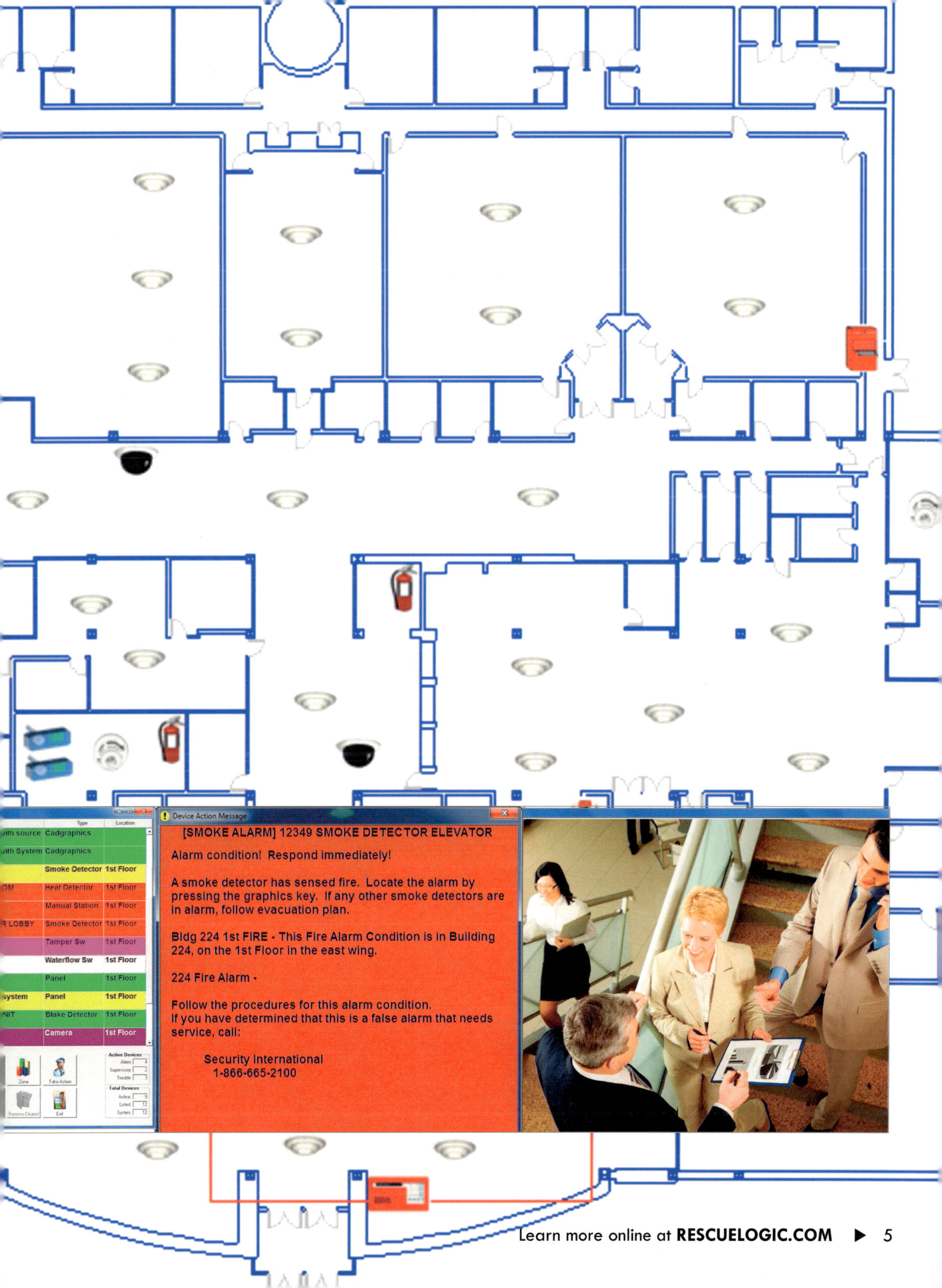
Type
Location
vith source Cadgraphics
vith System Cadgraphics
Smoke Detector 1st Floor
OM Heat Detector 1st Floor
Manual Station 1st Floor
R LOBBY Smoke Detector 1st Floor
Tamper Sw 1st Floor
Waterflow Sw 1st Floor
Panel 1st Floor
system Panel 1st Floor
NIT Blake Detector 1st Floor
Camera 1st Floor
Active Devices
Zone
Take Action
Total Devices
Exit
Device Action Message
[SMOKE ALARM] 12349 SMOKE DETECTOR ELEVATOR
Alarm condition! Respond immediately!
A smoke detector has sensed fire. Locate the alarm by pressing the graphics key. If any other smoke detectors are in alarm, follow evacuation plan.
Bldg 224 1st FIRE - This Fire Alarm Condition is in Building 224, on the 1st Floor in the east wing.
224 Fire Alarm -
Follow the procedures for this alarm condition.
If you have determined that this is a false alarm that needs service, call:
Security International
1-866-665-2100

The inspiration and innovation behind RescueLogic

RescueLogic makes it easy to monitor building safety and security from a standard personal computer — and it's been tried, tested, and proven to work by customers just like you, all around the world.

Our company's founder, Dan Horon, was a fledgling fire protection engineer when he decided to use AutoCAD to show fire alarms on a floor plan. His idea was a stroke of innovation, imagination, and inspiration.

Horon's invention immediately solved a whole host of problems. Before he introduced his software, it was almost impossible to update and monitor fire-alarm systems as buildings were updated and remodeled. Technicians and building managers were frustrated by alarm systems that combined hardware and devices from multiple manufacturers — most of which didn't communicate with each other, or work well in combination. And when alarms went off during tests, false alarms, or emergencies, security teams were forced to analyze confusing numeric data, assess events on the fly, and create service records and reports by hand.

Horon started selling the software by word of mouth, to customers who were serious about managing their facilities. He developed a simple plug-and-play import function to get data from alarm systems and devices, as well as an intuitive drag-and-drop process for showing them on maps and floor plans. The software even works with building control systems. In fact, it's an ingenious tool for total facility management alerts.

For years, Horon sold the software as Cadgraphics. The newest version of the software, RescueLogic, integrates fully with the industry's most popular fire and security alarms, panels, devices, and networks — and it works with standard computers, laptops, printers, and cell phones.

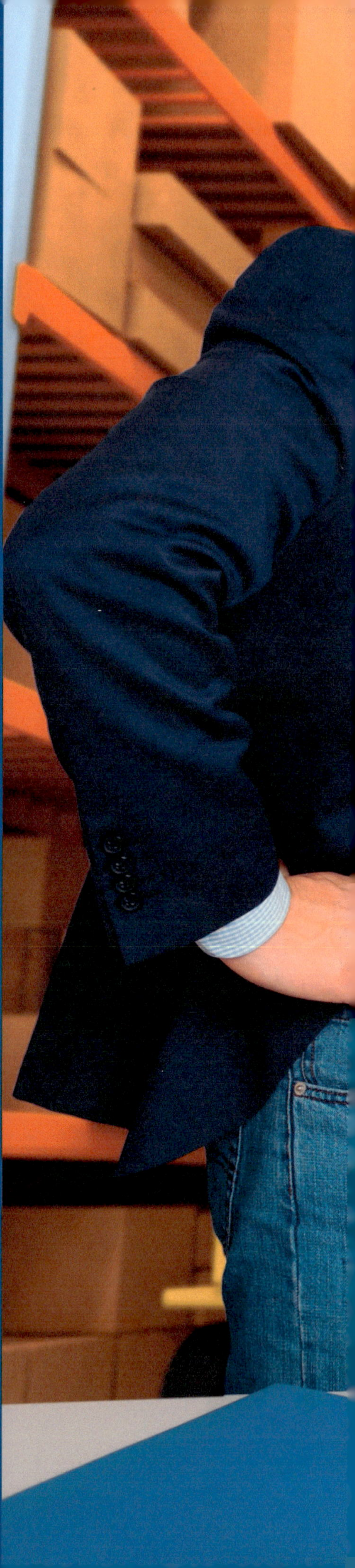

RESCUE**LOGIC**®
SOFTWARE BY CADGRAPHICS®

Nine panels, five buildings, and one sweet fire system

The makers of an artificial sweetener in the southern U.S. have a wide range of safety equipment in place — including nine different fire panels from five manufacturers, housed in nine separate buildings.

Facility managers needed to manage the fire and security systems that were sprinkled accross the campus. With RescueLogic software, they now monitor all nine buildings from a single personal computer.

The simple, streamlined interface tracks a wide range of fire-alarm devices, including waterflow switches, smoke detectors, pull stations, tamper switches, horns, strobe lights, and speakers.

RescueLogic works with today's most popular fire, security, and building control systems. RescueLogic also works with standard personal computers, laptops, touch-screen computers, and printers.

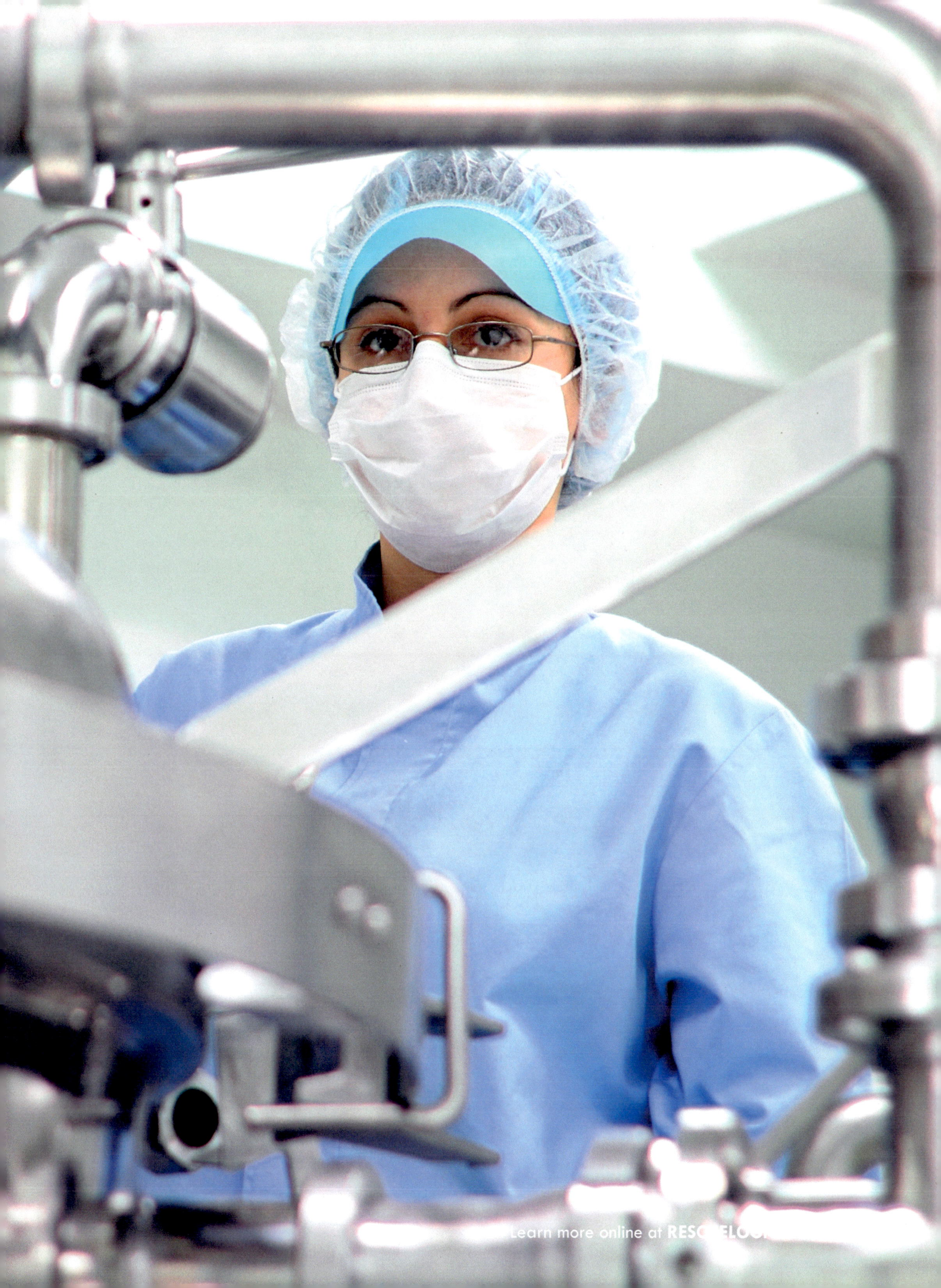
Learn more online at RESC

A state-of-the-art upgrade gives new life to old gear

Building managers at a midwest production plant found themselves in real trouble when the facility's central receiving station went down, and they lost their ability to monitor alarms and safety equipment.

Those alarms were critical: almost 1,000 people work at the site, in nine buildings on a campus that's more than a century old. The site's safety equipment had been pieced together over many years, and obsolete parts couldn't be replaced.

The plant's fire-alarm installer called Cadgraphics, and within days, facility managers were back in control of their safety system. They simply abandoned their dedicated network wiring and replaced the outdated front-end system with RescueLogic software.

The short-term fix gave them the time they needed to make long-term improvements. Within two months they actually replaced all their alarm panels and systems with current technology.

They didn't replace their RescueLogic system, though. As each new component went on line, the RescueLogic database was automatically updated, ensuring that facility managers could keep a watchful eye on their site for years to come.

Emergency alerts by email keep you up to date

RescueLogic software helps ensure that decision makers and key personnel always know the status of their sites. That way, facilities don't go unprotected when key personnel go home.

A wide range of hospitals, telecommunication centers, processing plants, and factories use the RescueLogic "Mail Dispatcher" add-on feature to send automatic email alerts whenever alarms and devices go into trouble or alarm. An optional GPS feature provides detailed maps and directions to any alarm's location.

Site managers can evaluate complex situations quickly, wherever they happen to be — and in the process, they save time, money, property, and lives.

A higher degree of safety for a major college campus

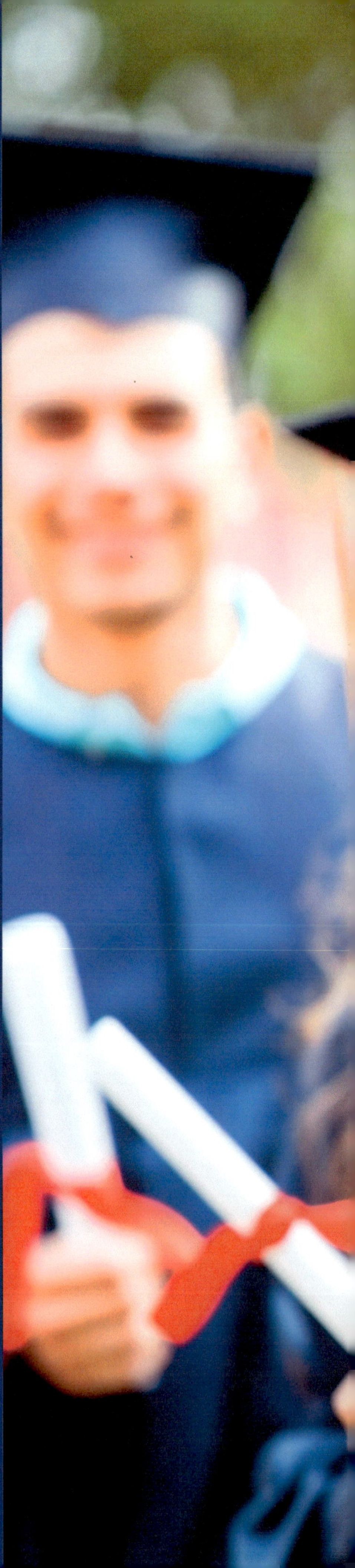

At one of the country's largest private universities, more than 200 buildings are spread out across 8,000 acres. The school even has its own police department and fire prevention group.

Campus safety managers wanted to supervise all of their alarms simultaneously, but the system wasn't networked — and the university didn't have copper or fiber communication lines to provide a dedicated backbone for a networked alarm system.

School administrators turned to RescueLogic, which had a turnkey solution for the site. Technicians simply added basic Ethernet modules to the buildings' control panels. With that one adjustment, they could use RescueLogic to monitor all of the alarm systems using the university's IP network.

Now first responders can access detailed alarm information during maintenance and emergencies, without installing an expensive, outdated network of dedicated phone lines or fiber optic cables.

Preserving the past for future generations

A well-known museum on the eastern seaboard is actually a five-building complex, complete with facilities the public rarely sees — like historical archives, scientific research labs, and secure storage areas.

Every area is linked to monitoring equipment, including IP cameras, temperature and humidity sensors, building automation controls, and emergency equipment. The museum has more than 2,000 sensors online — many of which send a constant stream of data to the museum's RescueLogic system.

The museum director and facility manager monitor that information from their desks and a guard station. They've also programmed their RescueLogic system to send individual emails to department managers and building tenants whenever specific devices go into trouble or alarm — so if artifacts are in danger of water damage, or a researcher's experiment is in jeopardy, they'll have time to save their work.

RESCUE**LOGIC**®
SOFTWARE BY CADGRAPHICS®

RescueLogic TV: When dead air isn't an option

For global television networks that broadcast 24 hours a day, a fully monitored alarm system is a must. Production schedules are timed to the second. Live broadcasts can't go off the air. Newscasters, program hosts, and celebrity guests can't leave the studio for a false alarm. Even a momentary shutdown can be devastating, because viewers will change channels and stations will lose millions of dollars in advertising revenue.

That's why some of the world's biggest sports and lifestyle networks use RescueLogic software to monitor alarms in their studios and production facilities. They watch their fire and security systems constantly, so they can stay on the air — and the rest of us can keep watching the show.

RESCUE**LOGIC**®
SOFTWARE BY CADGRAPHICS®

Airport maps and travel guides for first responders

Sprawling modern airports can be difficult places to navigate — even for employees behind the scenes.

The fire department at one of the nation's busiest airports has relied on Cadgraphics for more than 10 years, with RescueLogic stations at the 911 emergency center, the alarm engineer's desk, the fire chief's office, and the fireman's pole.

In 2012, the airport fire department was the first to implement RescueLogic's new GPS feature. During emergencies, it automatically sends email notifications to firefighters, who receive those emails on their cell phones.

With one click, they can see the exact location of more than 7,000 alarms. They can get maps, driving directions, and pedestrian routes to the site. They can even see which entrances they should use, and they can know whether airport traffic will impede their travel.

When there's trouble in the terminal or on the tarmac, first responders rely on RescueLogic.

SPEED
LIMIT
20
UNLOAD
ONLY
LOAD

RESCUE**LOGIC**®
SOFTWARE BY CADGRAPHICS®

Safeguarding store data for a worldwide retailer

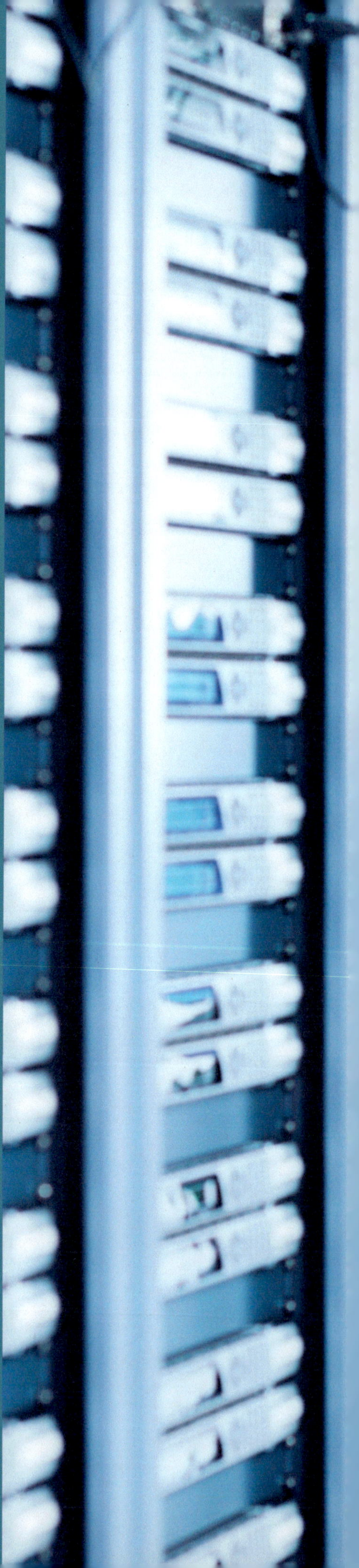

One of the world's largest retailers — a chain store that serves millions of customers each week, in dozens of countries around the world — tracks all of its business resources from a computer data center at its global headquarters.

The center's databank keeps complete records of each store and warehouse's inventories, as well as cash-register accounts, staff reports, and employee records. That information is so valuable that the retailer actually built a second, redundant data center to back up its computer files — and it safeguards both of them with RescueLogic software.

The RescueLogic system is largely dedicated to fire detection and suppression. It monitors spot smoke detectors under a raised floor and at the ceiling, as well as VESDA smoke detectors that pull smoke in through a network of sampling tubes.

RescueLogic software is an economical way to protect billions of dollars in sales.

RESCUE**LOGIC**®
SOFTWARE BY CADGRAPHICS®

Attention all personnel: Audible emergency alerts

More than 1,000 people work in an American paper mill that manufactures some of the most recognized products in the world, including tissues and paper towels. Managers at the mill wanted a reliable way to broadcast audible emergency messages over the public-address system — so they turned to Cadgraphics' software.

Originally, facility managers had relied on voice evacuation alerts that had come with their fire alarm system. Unfortunately, before the system was even completely installed, they realized that the system didn't have enough memory capacity for all the messages they wanted to play.

Cadgraphics developed a custom application that's now available to every other customer — the RescueLogic "Announcer" program. Now administrators have the ability to broadcast a virtually unlimited number of emergency alerts. They can even mix and match message segments to create variations of each alert, customized by the type, condition, and location of alarms and monitoring equipment.

RESCUE**LOGIC**®
SOFTWARE BY CADGRAPHICS®

Quiet healing spaces for children and their families

Like most hospitals, a well-known children's hospital was constantly being remodeled and reconfigured. Typically, portions of the fire alarm system would be disabled while some areas and zones were under construction. False alarms were a problem — especially for caregivers in the pediatric intensive care unit, where children couldn't be evacuated without upsetting patients and parents alike.

Over the course of 20 years, the hospital's alarm system had undergone major changes. During that time, new alarms and new panels from several manufacturers had been added to the system, and hundreds of alarm devices that were listed on spreadsheets were inaccurate.

RescueLogic helped heal the system, almost overnight. The hospital's maintenance engineer simply worked with the IT department to connect each of the hospital's alarm panels to RescueLogic, which automatically learned about each device installed.

Now the hospital uses RescueLogic to schedule maintenance on the alarm system, so that areas of the hospital that aren't under construction stay fully protected. Building managers can also add notes to the RescueLogic system about which contractors are in the building, as well as their timelines and their contact information.

Say it in Spanish: RescueLogic speaks your language

In an emergency, you need to communicate quickly and clearly. But if you speak English, and your security team speaks Spanish, words may fail you — with disastrous results.

RescueLogic can help you bridge the language gap, because RescueLogic can communicate in *any* language.

In fact, RescueLogic has even published a free guide to the Spanish words and phrases you'll need to set up a bilingual RescueLogic system.

The handbook, *Say It in Spanish,* includes hundreds of terms that are commonly used in fire, security, and facility management. You can use it when you set up your system's maps and floor plans, and you can follow its suggestions for a wide range of emergency "Take Action" instructions.

Try it, and you'll discover that RescueLogic truly is "safety made simple" — *seguridad simplificada.*

RESCUE**LOGIC**®
SOFTWARE BY CADGRAPHICS®

Customize your RescueLogic system with extra features

Every RescueLogic system comes ready to collect and interpret data from the panels and devices on your site. You can also customize your RescueLogic system with additional features, including:

- **SYSTEM WATCH** to monitor your system from a remote computer
- **ACTIVITY REPORTS** to compile printable records of system activity
- **MAIL DISPATCHER** to send automatic email alerts of alarms
- **REPLICATOR** to make a live backup of your event database
- **ANNOUNCER** to add voice messages to your public address system
- **VERBALERT** to add audible alerts for your security team

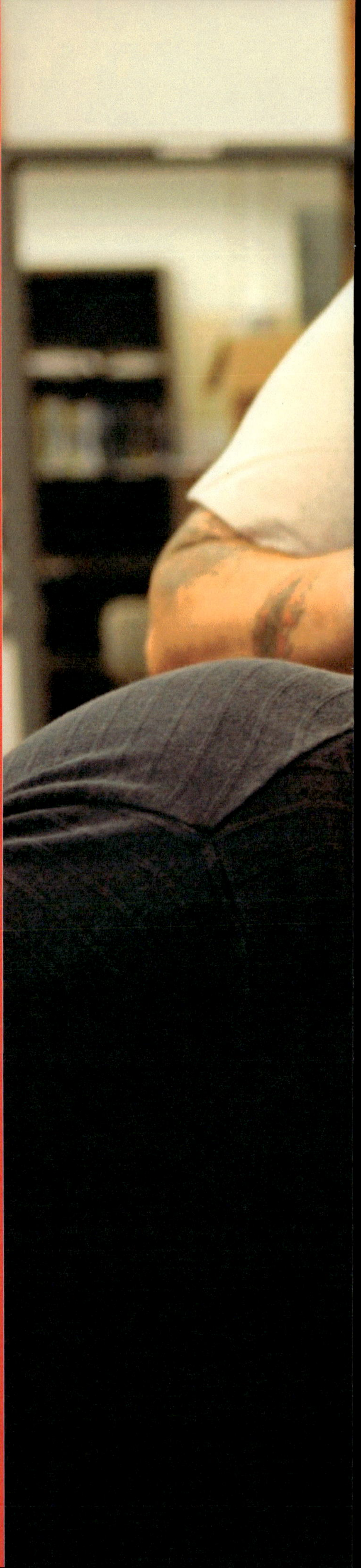

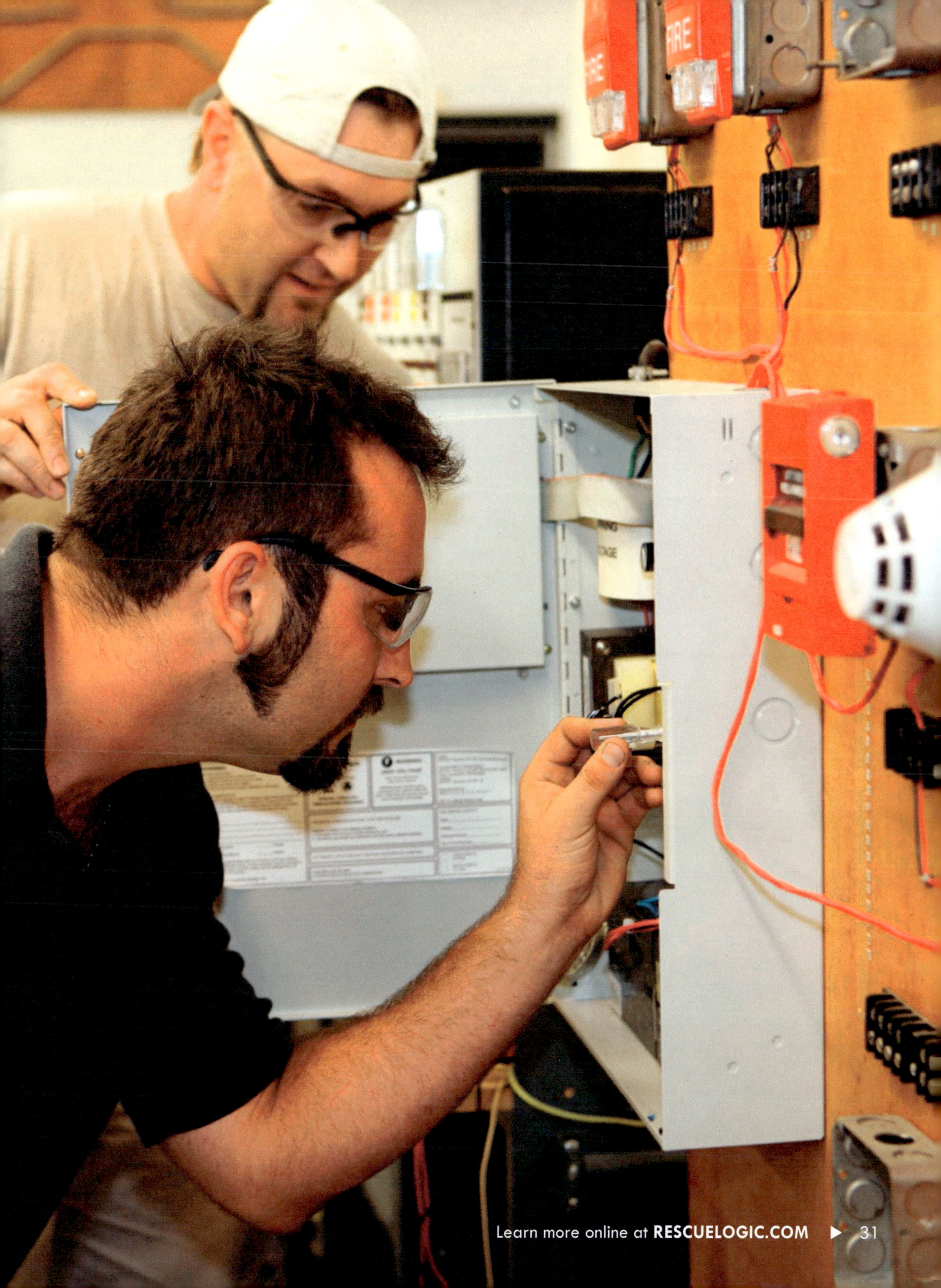
FIRE
FIRE

RESCUE**LOGIC**®
SOFTWARE BY CADGRAPHICS®

RescueLogic software puts you in good company

ADM
Aflac
Ahold
AK Steel
Alcoa
Alison Control Inc.
Allergan
Allina Hospitals & Clinics
Ameritech
AT&T
Bank of America
BASF
BellSouth Communications
Boeing
Bolthouse Farms
California State University
Capital One
Chicago Stock Exchange
Coca-Cola
ComEd
ConocoPhillips
Dell
Delphi
Delta Airlines
Deutsche Bank
Duke University
DuPont
Eli Lilly
ESPN
Exxon Mobil
Fidelity Investments
Harvard's Field Museum
Firestone
Freddie Mac
General Dynamics
GoDaddy
Goldman Sachs
Goodyear
Google
Hilton
Home Depot
IKEA
Iron Mountain
Johnson & Johnson
Kerr-McGee
Kimberly-Clark
Kirtland AFB
Lear Corporation
Levi Straus
Liberty University
Lifescan
Lockheed-Martin
Lucent Technologies
Macy's
MasterCard
Mayo Clinics
MCI

Medtronic
Mercedes Benz
Merck
Miami Dade County
Michigan State University
Microsoft
Mills Pride
Monroe Shocks
National Institute of Standards and Technology
National Oceanic and Atmospheric Administration
Nationwide Insurance
Nestle Purina
New York Hospital
New York Life
Nokia
Northrop Grumman
NutraSweet
Oracle
Pacific Bell
Pepsico
Planet Hollywood
PNC Park
Port of Seattle
Remann Detention
Riyadh Village, Saudi Arabia
San Diego Gas & Electric
San Jose Civic Center
SAPPI Fine Paper
Savvis Communications
Scotiabank
Scripps Networks (HGTV & DIY)
Seagate
Sidwell Friends
Sony
Southwestern Bell
Sprint
T-Mobile
Toyota
Unilever
U.S. Army
Unisys
United Airlines
United Nations in Liberia
University of Pennsylvania
University of Utah
Verizon
Victoria's Secret
Victory Base Camp Iraq
VISA
Wal-Mart Stores, Inc.
Wells Fargo
Westinghouse
Yahoo!

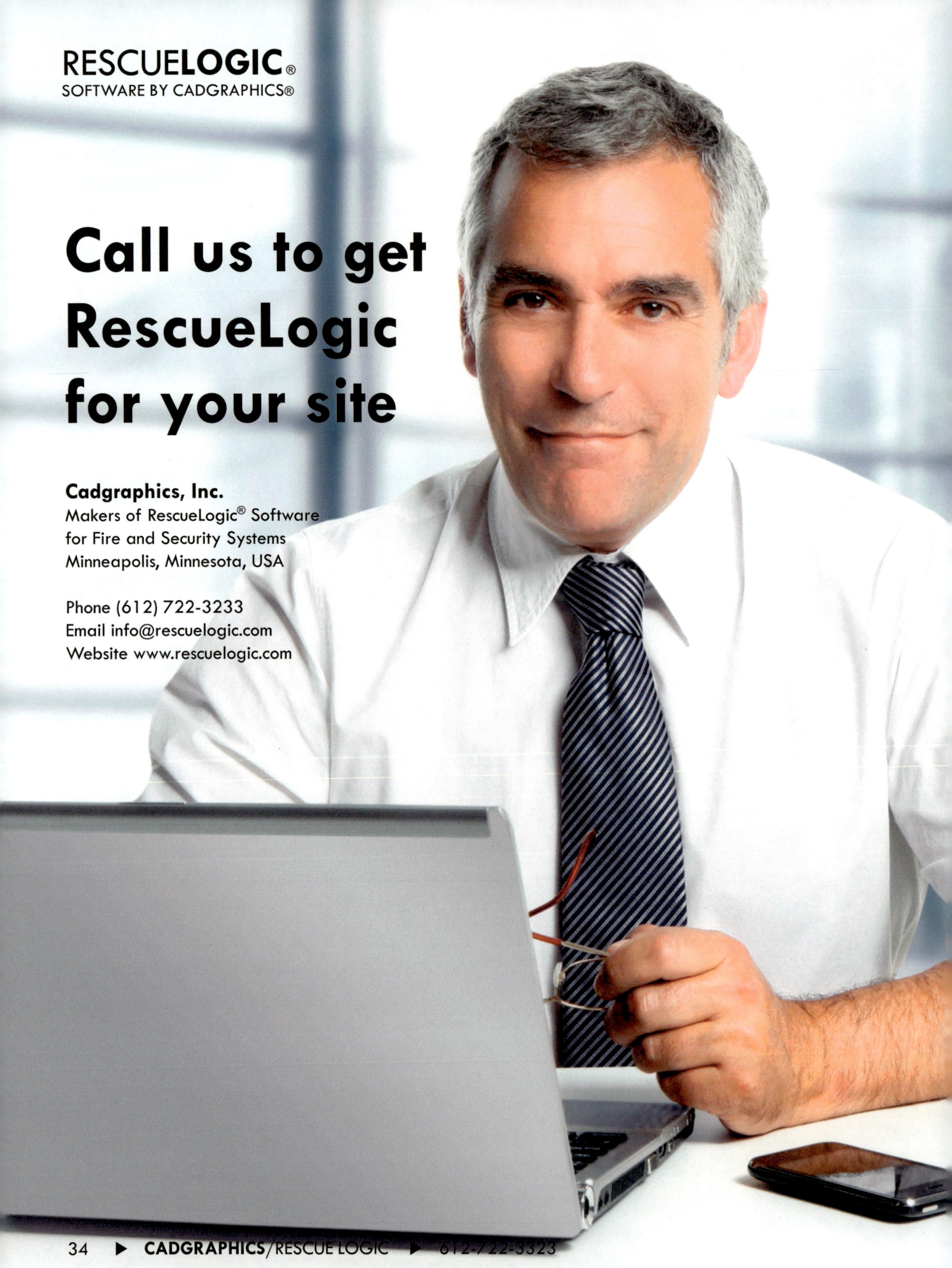
RESCUELOGIC®
SOFTWARE BY CADGRAPHICS®
Call us to get RescueLogic for your site
Cadgraphics, Inc.
Makers of RescueLogic® Software
for Fire and Security Systems
Minneapolis, Minnesota, USA
Phone (612) 722-3233
Email info@rescuelogic.com
Website www.rescuelogic.com